SMITH
BLUE

CRAB ORCHARD SERIES IN POETRY / OPEN COMPETITION AWARD

SMITH
BLUE

Camille T. Dungy

CRAB ORCHARD REVIEW &
SOUTHERN ILLINOIS UNIVERSITY PRESS
CARBONDALE

24 23 22 21   11 10 9 8

The Crab Orchard Series in Poetry is a joint publishing venture
of Southern Illinois University Press and *Crab Orchard Review*.
This series has been made possible by the generous support
of the Office of the President of Southern Illinois University
and the Office of the Vice Chancellor for Academic Affairs and
Provost at Southern Illinois University Carbondale.

Crab Orchard Series in Poetry Editor: Jon Tribble
Open Competition Award Judge for 2010: Michael Waters

Library of Congress Cataloging-in-Publication Data
Dungy, Camille T., 1972–
Smith blue / Camille T. Dungy.
    p. cm. — (The Crab Orchard series in poetry)
ISBN-13: 978-0-8093-3031-7 (pbk. : alk. paper)
ISBN-10: 0-8093-3031-8 (pbk. : alk. paper)
ISBN-13: 978-0-8093-8633-8 (ebook)
ISBN-10: 0-8093-8633-X (ebook)
I. Title.
PS3604.U538S65 2011
811'.6—dc22   2010041206

Printed on recycled paper. ♻

For Ray

Contents

X

X

Acknowledgments

Poems in this volume first appeared in the following publications:

"After Opening the *New York Times* I Wonder How to Write a Poem about Love" and "Maybe Tuesday Will Be My Good News Day" in *Drunken Boat*

"Daisy Cutter" in *Washington, D.C. Poets against the War*, 2nd edition; reprinted on *From the Fishouse*

"A Massive Dying Off" in *Parthenon West Review*

"Emergency Plan" and "My Lover Who Lives Far" in *Electronic Poetry Review*

"The Way We Carry On" in *The LBJ*

"Association Copy" in *The Melic Review*

"On Ice" in *Hawk and Handsaw: The Journal of Creative Sustainability*

"Flight" in *Natural Bridge*

"The Blue" on *The Rumpus*

"Prayer for P——": section I in *Pebble Lake Review*; section IV in *Connotation Press*; section V in *Ninth Letter*

"Since Everyone Can Never Be Safe" in *Runes: A Review of Poetry*; reprinted in *Black Nature: Four Centuries of African American Nature Poetry*

"Arthritis is one thing, the hurting another" in *MiPOesias*; reprinted in *Letters to the World: Poems from the Womp-po Listserve*

"It Is" and "That's a State I'll Never Go Back To" in *The American Poetry Review*

"Ease" and "On the Rocks" in *Cave Wall*

"Something about Grandfathers" in *New Pony: A Horse Less Anthology*

"Her mother sings warning of the new world" in *Torch*

"Five for Truth" and "How She Keeps Faith" in *Weber: The Contemporary West*

"*The Little Building in which I Find the Ancient Cloister Store-room of St. Severin, which is Going to Disappear*" in *The Yalobusha Review*

"before her heart, a mechanical aperture, closed" in *Lo-Ball*

"Out of the Darkness" in *West Branch*

"How She Keeps Faith" was commissioned by the Rocky Mountain National Park Artist-in-Residence program.

The writing of many of these poems has been supported by fellowships and awards from the National Endowment for the Arts, the Virginia Commission for the Arts, the American Antiquarian Society, the Corporation of Yaddo, the Rocky Mountain National Park Artist-in-Residence Program, the Ragdale Foundation, the Norton Island/Eastern Frontier Society, the Virginia Center for the Creative Arts, the Bread Loaf Writers' Conference, Cave Canem, Randolph-Macon Woman's College, and San Francisco State University.

Thanks to Michael Waters for choosing this book and to Jon Tribble for his keen editor's eye. I also owe deep gratitude to James Hoch, Shara McCallum, Shane Book, Ravi Shankar, and Lucy Anderton for their concentrated time, care, and support as I composed and revised the poems gathered here. There are those whose comments, though not always intended for my poems, I applied to my poems. This number includes, but is not limited to, Rita Dove, Fred Viebahn, D. A. Powell, Stephen Burt, Alan Shapiro, Leslie Kirk Campbell, Steve Dickison, Scott Cardwell, my most engaging students, my most astute friends, my most articulate family, my workshop companions, my retreat companions, my husband, my dreaming self. And to all those who go unnamed, the spinners of linen, the keepers of trees, the pressers of paper, the tenders of my body, the bearers of my food, ashe, selah, thank you.

Let us combine. There are no magic or elves
Or timely godmothers to guide us. We are lost, must
Wizard a track through our own screaming weed.
                    —Gwendolyn Brooks

What elegy is, not loss but opposition.
                    —C. D. Wright

After Opening the *New York Times* I Wonder
How to Write a Poem about Love

To love like God can love, sometimes.
Before the kettle boils to a whistle, quiet. Quiet
that is lost on me, waiting as I am
for an alarm. The sort of things I notice:
the bay over redbud blossoms, mountains
over magnolia blooms. There is always something
starting somewhere, and I have lost ambition
to look into the details. Shame fits comfortably
as my best skirt, and what can I do
but walk around in that habit? Turn the page.
Turn another page. This was meant to be
about love. Now there is nothing left but this.

X

Daisy Cutter

Pause here at the flower stand—mums
and gladiolas, purple carnations

dark as my heart. We are engaged
in a war, and I want to drag home

any distraction I can carry. Tonight
children will wake to bouquets of fire

that will take their breath away. Still,
I think of my life. The way you hold me,

sometimes, you could choke me.
There is no way to protect myself,

except by some brilliant defense. I want
the black iris with their sabered blooms.

I want the flamethrowers: the peonies,
the sunflowers. I will cut down the beautiful ones

and let their nectared sweetness bleed
into the careless air. This is not the world

I'd hoped it could be. It is horrible,
the way we carry on. Last night, you catalogued

our arsenal. You taught me devastation
is a goal we announce in a celebration

of shrapnel. Our bombs shower
in anticipation of their marks. You said this

is to assure damage will be widely distributed.
What gruesome genius invents our brutal hearts?

When you touch me I am a stalk of green panic
and desire. Wait here while I decide which

of these sprigs of blossoming heartbreak I can afford
to bring into my home. Tonight dreams will erupt

in chaotic buds of flame. This is the world we have
arranged. It is horrible, this way we carry on.

A Massive Dying Off

When the fish began their dying you didn't worry.

      You bought new shoes.
            They looked like crocodiles:
snappy and rich,
      brown as delta mud.

           Even the box they shipped in was beautiful, bejeweled.

      You tore through masses of swaddling paper,
         these shoes!

       carefully cradled
in all that cardboard by what
         you now understand
must have been someone's tiny, indifferent hands.

       *

The five-fingered sea stars you heard about on NPR.

You must have been driving to Costco.
It must have been before all the visitors arrived.

You needed covers, pillows, disposable containers.
At Costco, everything comes cheap.

Sea stars, jellies, anemones, all the scuttlers and hoverers
and clingers along the ocean floor. *A massive dying off, further displacing
depleted oxygen,* cried the radio announcer.

You plugged in your iPod.
Enough talk. You'd found the song you had been searching for.

*

One cargo ship going out. One cargo ship coming in.

Crabs crawling up trawler lines.
Giant lobsters walking
right onto the shore.

You've been sitting in your car
watching the sunset over the Golden Gate.
NPR again.

One cargo ship going out. One cargo ship coming in.

Those who can are leaving.

The Marin Headlands crouch
toward the ocean,
fog so thick on their side of the bay
you can't tell crag from cloud from sea.

One cargo ship headed out, another coming in.

They're looking for a place
where they can breathe.

You've been here less than an hour.
When the sun has finished setting
you'll go home.

*

In the dream, your father is the last refuse to wash ashore.
This wasn't what you wanted.
Any of you.
The first sign

of trouble was the bottle with the message.
    That washed up years ago.
Then, so many bottles
        the stenographers couldn't answer all the messages anymore.

          The women of the village wept when your father died.

Then they lined up to deliver tear-stained tissue to the secretary of the interior
    who translated their meaning
and had it writ out on a scroll.

These were the answers your people had been waiting for!

       That papyrus wound around your father like a bandage.
    The occasion announced,
       you prayed proper prayers, loaded him onto an outrigger,
set him off,
            but here he is again. Stinking.
    Swelling.

You can't dispose of the rising dead and you're worried.
    What can you do?

Emergency Plan

First we decided where to meet.
The fire was coming and I knew

what we would need: flashlights,
water, condoms, and a shot

of our imaginary son. Only, what we used to call *our*
peeping birds startled me into starting days

long before the city bus commenced its run.
That's when I knew we hadn't done enough

in case the sky fell while I was driving,
and I packed a pair of panties, matches,

some aspirin in the trunk. After we stopped
making breakfast plans (the pecking

woke me early and by breakfast
I was always eating lunch), I secreted

in my office that little blue box:
trail mix, shekels, and seed to plant

after the revolution was over
and done. I made sure we remembered

where we planned to meet, taught us
to swim in case we came near water

when it decided to flood. But those damned birds
with their nesting scattered on the patio

were eventually the most reliable alarm,
and, only to level the threat, I fashioned a carryall

from the pillowcase I no longer slept on.
I filled it: tinned meat and crackers, chocolate,

a little musk so I can recall
how we smelled before this end was begun.

Association Copy

Lynda Hull

Maybe you sold it to buy junk. Though I like to think not.
And I don't want to think you used the money for food
or rent or anything obligatory, practical.
A pair of boots, perhaps. Thigh high burgundy boots
with gold laces. Something crucial as lilies.
Mostly, I want to believe you held onto the book,
that your fingers brailed those pages' inky veins
even in your final weeks. I want to believe
words can be that important in the end.

Who can help the heart, which is grand and full
of gestures? I had been on my way out.
He was rearranging his bookshelves
when, in an approximation of tenderness,
he handed me, like the last of the sweet potatoes
at Thanksgiving, like a thing he wanted
but was willing to share, the rediscovered book—
he'd bought it years ago in a used bookstore
in Chicago. Levine's poems, with your signature inside.

That whole year I spent loving him, something splendid
as lemons, sour and bright and leading my tongue
toward new language, was on the shelf. These
weren't your own poems, autographed, a stranger's
souvenir—we'd spent vain months leafing through
New York stacks for your out-of-print collections—but you'd cared
about this book, or cared enough to claim it, your name
looped across the title page as if to say, *Please.*

This is mine. This book is mine. Though you sold it.
Or someone else did when you died.

We make habits out of words. I grew accustomed
to his, the way they spooned me into sleep
so many times. Now I am sleepless and alone
another night. What would you give for one more night
alone? No booze. No drugs. Just that hunger
and those words. He gave me *The Names of the Lost*.
Need comes down hard on a body. What else
was sold? What else—do you know?—did we lose?

On Ice

As if the ice rose from the sea
                                unborn, and ice begat ice
                which bore ice which begat ice
                                and on through the ages,
near absolute south
                                there were islands
glaciered so thickly there was no discerning
                        the land of the island beneath. Ice
                                smooth as an egg. Ice smooth
                                as an egg with a hole
                                        like the bird's just hatching.
                Ice smooth as an egg
                        with cracks like the bird's furious, hatching.
                                Bits of ice
scattering the channel
                as if the bird hatched and was gone.
                        Ice—I remember ice—
like a mucous membrane—
                something monstrous, gelatinous, just up from the lab—
ice like a liver-spotted lung.
                                Five, four, three, none: Scott's tardy polar party
                        sledged far too slowly north
over eight hundred miles of ice.
                                Evans felled by a glacier,
                                Oates martyred in a blizzard,
                                later, a cairn for the last three, of snow
                and of ice. Plateaus. Rivers of ice. Ice fields. Cliffs
of ice, their sheer faces far taller than ships.

Millennia of ice
on millennia of ice. Snow,
frozen in time,
carbuncling cliff faces. Ice fastened
in crags of iced-over mountains.
Ice heaped forty feet at the top

—and just the top—
of volcanic peaks, decadent. Insane, but not unbalanced,
when Oates went—
I'm just going outside
and I may be some time—after the limping
on ice and the dying, he went into ice.
Great caverns of ice,
great crevasses. Ice
bridges: some are fast, some fail.

Flight

It is the day after the leaves, when buckeyes,
like a thousand thousand pendulums, clock trees,
and squirrels, fat in their winter fur, chuckle hours,
chortle days. It is the time for the parting of our ways.

You slid into the summer of my sleeping, crept
into my lonely hours, ate the music of my dreams.
You filled yourself with the treated sweet I offered,
then shut your rolling eyes and stole my sleep.

Came morning and me awake. Came morning.
Awake, I walked twelve miles to the six-gun shop.
On the way there I saw a bird-of-prayer all furled up by the river.
I called to it. It would not unfold. On the way home I killed it.

It is the time of the waking cold, when buckeyes,
like a thousand thousand metronomes, tock time,
and you, fat on my summer sleep, titter toward me,
walk away. It is the time for the parting of our days.

The Blue

One will live to see the Caterpillar rut everything
they walk on—seacliff buckwheat cleared, relentless
ice plant to replace it, the wild fields bisected
by the scenic highway, canyons covered with cul-de-sacs,
gas stations, comfortable homes, the whole habitat
along this coastal stretch endangered, everything,
everyone, everywhere in it in danger as well—
but now they're logging the one stilling hawk
Smith sights, the conspiring grasses' shh shhhh ssh,
the coreopsis Mattoni's boot barely spares,
and, netted, a solitary blue butterfly. Smith
ahead of him chasing the stream, Mattoni wonders
if he plans to swim again. Just like that
the spell breaks. It's years later, Mattoni lecturing
on his struggling butterfly. How fragile.

            *

If his daughter spooled out the fabric
she's chosen for her wedding gown,
raw taffeta, burled, a bright-hued tan,
perhaps Mattoni would remember
how those dunes looked from a distance,
the fabric, balanced between her arms,
making valleys in the valley, the fan
above her mimicking the breeze.
He and his friend loved everything

softly undulating under the coyest wind,
and the rough truth as they walked
through the land's scratch and scrabble
and no one was there, then, besides Mattoni
and his friend, walking along Dolan's Creek,
in that part of California they hated
to share. The ocean, a mile or so off,
anything but passive so that even there,
in the canyon, they sometimes heard it smack
and pull well-braced rocks. The breeze,
basic: salty, bitter, sour, sweet. Smith trying
to identify the scent, tearing leaves
of manzanita, yelling, "This is it. Here! This is it!"
his hand to his nose, his eyes, having finally seen
the source of his pleasure, alive.

*

In the lab, after the accident, he remembered it,
the butterfly. How good a swimmer Smith had been,
how rough the currents there at Half Moon Bay, his friend
alone with reel and rod—Mattoni back at school
early that year, his summer finished too soon—
then all of them together in the sneaker wave,
and before that the ridge, congregations of pinking
blossoms, and one of them bowing, scaring up the living,
the frail and flighty beast too beautiful
to never be pinned, those nights Mattoni worked
without his friend, he remembered too.
He called the butterfly Smith's Blue.

The Way We Carry On

There is the sky. Shhh. It might go soon
and then where will we be? Purple
and all over with blue. This temperate sky
will not comfort you some day, I think
you told me and mine, who were, as now, crouching
stands of crocuses. Too early yet! Too early for all this
springing. Am I wrong? Who would say that
to me then? Come here. Come over here
and see what the bird's nest is doing.
There are these small eggs, all of these
small eggs, none of them cracked yet,
but the big bird's away. I told you it might go.

Prayer for P——

After C. P. Cavafy

I.

The door even,
her apartment door,
even her door

suffered cruelly. Was it not
enough no one knocked
all that time? Even her lover

tore inside, afraid
of who might see him—
owing to the fact his wife,
kids, were too important

to lose over this piece,
he came and went, feeling
entitled to hurry, needing to

screw her and be done,
and he had to give her that,
instead of begging him to stay she let him
leave her when he needed—
other women made it difficult,
reducing his desire, but she took it,

incredible, really, what she took,
never complaining, not even asking
that he knock. Rather, she waited,
opened the door before he need bother—

inside, it would be just as easy, he thought
this is what kept him coming, she was not
so beautiful, but he found something

desirable in that, in her
eagerness to bring him inside. And so
perhaps he is the most surprised among us
to hear what the men had to do,
how they carried her away, but not before
shattering the door, breaking it down off its hinges.

II.

None of us know what to do about death. Untimely death
or prolonged illness, neither is easy
to handle. When her mother failed she thought it would be useful

knowing she'd established directions to turn, certain safety
nets, support she could depend on if
only for some time. She refused to be at a loss, struggling
without words. So when her mother died (dying, dying, dead), she sought
inspiration: *After I buried my mother I would see her often.* Words
netted her. For years they trussed and delivered her. We couldn't
grant enough praise for her haunting dirges. Though we considered her

trapped by death, held in thrall by her mother,
her dying, we let her go on. Never said enough now,
enough. Bury that story. Move on. We pitied her because we knew her

mother's death had been hard. After all the grief she was
obviously alone. Who wants a child
touched by death? We pitied her because we knew, we thought,
how she must have needed us. So
everyone, when called upon, had something
ready to say about whatever she put down:

graceful, we used to cry, incredible,
on and on we'd laud, tossing clumps of praise,
enthralling, we'd call her poems,
simply unforgettable, perfect,

beautiful, we'd proclaim until,

exhausting ourselves, we broke apart,

fumbled on, as we all must,

opening doors and closing them, presenting our own bodies,

removing them (until we cannot,

everyone must), and in this way we carried our own hearts

through our days. We would see her sometimes and call,

how are you holding up? That was good enough. Good

enough for all of us, the way we talked to her. Sometimes.

Vexed and alone, she had no one. Then,

in everyone came rushing. Fine work, we'd say. This is how we got along:

ready, we thought, to say what was needed. We had no idea how to handle her,

grown child, grieving. Sometimes we left her alone. We said ta ta,

it's true. So long. When she died (not dead, then dead), no net, not a soul,

not a word, nothing but the ground came round to catch her.

III.

another thing, you've got to remember
not to forget to remember who to thank—
don't forget to remember, I should remind you,

let me remind you, everything you want to call your own,
it's not your own,
good god, don't forget
how you came by everything,
things you don't even know you have you have
simply because someone above you,

always above you,

took it in his heart to care for you,
and the least you can do,
let me remind you, is remember, don't be lazy
like I know you want to be, lazy like I know you

can be, lazy and careless when you think no one cares
about what you're getting up to,
no one should have to remind you,
don't forget you'd be nothing
left to your own devices, I don't want to have to remind you
everything you have you have because of someone above you

IV.

—for awhile things had been going well,
only an ungrateful woman would complain,
reaching, as ungrateful women reach,

higher than is warranted or right. I want this,
especially this, I want this
remembered: if ever anyone was grateful, P——was

best known for being grateful, for she was
always grateful. And of course she was grateful
because for so long everything had been going fairly well. I'm sure
you can understand why

this much I remember about her. This much
only, I'm afraid. But I'll claim

cartographer's liberties. I'll claim
omissions for the greater good. I am grateful
my imagination has been drafted for the greater good,
especially since what I mean to do is direct. I want to

be your guide. I have always been
afraid of steering someone incorrectly,
causing, by my own shortcoming, insufficient
knowledge, harm to another. It used to be they didn't know,

so in those parts they drew danger—sea scorpions, enormous
octopi, leviathan—but also wonders, rising suns. The open sea is just that,
open. My dictionary has sixty-four definitions for the word *open*,
none of them defining how I feel now, my heart

a little more open because without her,

not the memory of her, the knowledge, not the insubstantial

decoys my mind sets up in lieu of her, but without the woman,

friend, her embodied body, without her this space is a little more

open, and now I am left to consider if there be anything, any

rare thing that might invoke her. Who she was: marvelously

good. It used to be they didn't know America,

only some folks put their experience

on paper. Mostly *America* was a dream spoken, directing another

dream, directing another dream, directing another, and P——,

when she heard *America*, heard what she wanted—

even those old map makers wanted us to want,

almost as much as they wanted us to fear,

to get to the places beyond the places we know. This is the way,

how we have always found more. Years before, P—— followed directions

even though this meant crossing out, over the open,

rough sea. And, she was grateful, for awhile things went well . . .

V.

—and of course you won't let me see you
neglecting to serve, whatever that means,
don't let me catch you neglecting to serve,

a girl like you cannot afford to neglect,
let me remind you, a girl like you
won't get far in this world
alone, you're smart enough to know this, so don't neglect
your duty to others, I don't care what you do
so long as you're willing to help

keep things running as they should be running,
even if it means no sleep for you, paper cuts, less time
enjoying the party, even if it means staying in the back room
photocopying flyers until well past five, perhaps you have forgotten,
so let me make sure you have not forgotten, a girl like you

has to make herself useful, even if it is difficult,
especially if it is difficult, work,
remember, is rarely anything but difficult,

especially for a girl like you, but don't raise a fuss,
a girl like you should not raise a fuss,
reminding everyone of everything you do,

a girl like you should be happy, remember
lots of girls like you have nothing,
even if it's the worst kind of work, don't let me catch you
refusing it, what do you think, it will kill you
to roll up your sleeves? treat every job like something manageable,

treat even the hardest job like something manageable
or it will too quickly seem, even to you, unmanageable,

treat even the plunging of a toilet like a job
handcrafted to show off your skills, even running your boss's business,
even collating the committee's papers, no organization

would function without girls like you, remember
it's an honor to be able to help,
no matter what it means you have to do,
don't neglect that duty. it won't kill you to do as I say.

VI.

Birda Mae, Shirley, Pat, Anita, Jennifer, Helen, June—
until I fail to fill my book of names and numbers
this list of losses will go on,

why, I can't even name them all, I'm stopped short,
hopeless at the sound of so many: R——, P——, M——, A——, J——, E—— . . .
it seems, sometimes, this will be the only thing left to pass on,
leave to my daughter, only these names,
even the pictures will be useless too soon,

so many unlabeled, even the gifts the dead gave,
handed to me out of their own hands. Someone asks, What's this? What's that?
eventually, even what matters most, someone will no longer care for,

perhaps sooner, perhaps later, and things will be broken,
ruined, ignored. Even my book of names
and numbers, what will I do with my book of names and numbers? When,
yesterday, I ran across P——'s address—
speeding, I was speeding, to get a stack of mailing done

and, oh god, there she was—I would have paused, except I remembered I had
no time. And what should I have done? What
do I do with the names and numbers? When I felt the most

envy it was because I had already lost count and some woman told me she had
never seen a real live dead person before,
this is the truth. This is what she said to me in the presence of her first
real live dead person. I thought
everybody knew as much about losing as I knew about losing,
and she did, too, but there is always more about losing
to learn. She made me so angry, that woman,
so angry, making me covet her little loss. So

help me, I was overwhelmed when P—— got carried away and abandoned
everything: her knives and her dishes, plants, poems, pictures, telephone,
records, everything, everyone, linens, lovers even, her pen, her books, her name,

VII.

that's not how you take care of your heart, is it
how you pretend to take care of your heart?
even a thick girl like you should know

it's important to take care of your heart,
can't you control what you put in your mouth?
only a big man or maybe a girl what doesn't want
no man to take her seriously would put so much in her mouth

let yourself get fat, why don't you? put that in your mouth, but know
it's no one's fault but yours what happens
soon as you let yourself go, you watch,
they'll blame everything on you, everything you
enjoy they'll recollect and turn against you,
no use pretending it's not true, no use eating
salad in company when we all know,

good god, you think we don't know? we know you
really want fried fish and everything else
all the people who know these things know
very well aren't even a little bit good for you, you eat
enough to fill up a big man or a fat girl

and you just wait, you might not need to wait too long,
no one will remember anything about you,
drop dead and all they'll say is but wasn't she fat?

seems to me she carried a lot of extra weight, *so, now, stop*
acting like a thick girl, be smart with your mouth,
don't tell me you don't know how to take care of your heart

VIII.

knowledge isn't always good, you know.
not knowing might be better. consider: *never* is
overwhelming when it's the answer
waiting for the question that must come:
it's been a long time since I saw my girl.
need to see my girl, I miss her.
girl, I miss you. when will I see you again?

that's something: *never*. that's really something
heavy to hoist. my friend was light. she was light
enough I hardly noticed her sometimes.

can't blame me. please, you can't blame me.
how could I be expected to always notice
if she was just that light? it's what her name meant:
light. it was the sound her voice made
drifting into smiles. light. she was so easy going

we took a long time to register her gone.
it was no one's fault, but she was alone sometimes,
left alone that last time how many days?
let's say four days. for four april days

no one needed anything from her. no one
except the strangers enlisted, finally, to carry her
very dead body out her door. listen,
even if I don't want to repeat this, I have to
repeat this. for four april days no one

recognized she was gone. there was no way to

escape telling you that. I tried to escape

telling you that. and now that I've told you it is

useless to hope to undo what's been done.

remember, she was my friend. don't let's forget, our friend.

not knowing, this was one awful thing. knowing, another.

Since Everyone Can Never Be Safe

The bitch ran in the pack
      and nothing about that was remarkable
      except the slick of her intestines on the ground.

But we were yakking about kids before we turned to dogs.
      They were playing, what d'you call that game?
Kids scattered in pairs across the yard, elbows linked, the lot of them,

      except the one who was it and one other one.
We worked fifty weeks a year now, adult hours.
These dinners: a decadence we could easily afford.

      The loose toms and spayed pups we called our own,
      even they knew there was more than enough
         and no longer beat us to the bowls we filled two times each day.

If the kid who's it's too close the other kid'll grab some arm.
      Then the kid whose partner got the grab,
now he's got to be the one to run.

My friend, she'd seen those dogs and, that night,
      though I'm sure we hadn't asked her,
      had to tell us about them.

The thing that got me was these kids,
they kept screaming,
      Trevor, Trevor, Trevor,

and holding out their arms.
Then it was Maria,
      Maria, Maria, *when Trevor grabbed someone.*

Most of us had been to the place she was talking about.
      God it was hot,
one of us remembered.

      Oh, and that flat bread!
We said, remember the west bank
      of the river? How lazy that afternoon was.

They'd yell, Maria, Maria,
and wave their little arms,
      though any arm that got the grab, that meant some other kid had to run.

      Dinner that night, if I can recall, consisted of several courses:
Lamb shank on a bed of cracked barley, chickpeas, home-cured olives,
      a chutney or two;

      arugula salad with cashews and organic tomatoes;
      thick-crusted bread; a healthy soup;
      something sweet to top it off; a plentitude of wine.

It was only the way she dragged herself along the street my friend
remembered. Like she was all together and not dripping apart.
      Not dragging her own stomach down the road.

It was only the way that bitch acted.

How normal she made all of it seem.

    Nothing remarkable. Those dogs. Their hunger.

I mean, what were they, really, what were they looking to do?

Even the way they consumed the bitch,

    those dogs.

My friend wanted us to see how easy it seemed,

watching all of this go down. That pack was unremarkable.

    She almost overlooked them, really.

    The way they got behind her and on top.

    That every one was eating.

Nothing could be less remarkable than that.

Arthritis is one thing, the hurting another

The poet's hands degenerate until her cup is too heavy.

You are not required to understand.
This is not the year for understanding.

This is the year of burning women in schoolyards
and raided homes, of tarped bodies on runways and in restaurants.

The architecture of the poet's hands has turned upon itself.

This is not the year for palliatives. It is not the year for knowing what to do.

This is the year the planet grew smaller
and no country would consent to its defeat.

The poet's cup is filled too full, a weight she cannot carry
from the table to her mouth, her lips, her tongue.
The poet's hands are congenitally spoiled.

This is not one thing standing for another.

Listen, this year three ancient cities met their ruin, maybe more,
and many profited, but this is not news for the readers here.

Should I speak indirectly?
I am not the poet. Those are not my hands.

This is the year of deportations and mothers bereaved
of all of their sons. The year of third and fourth tours,
of cutting-edge weaponry and old-fashioned guns.

Last year was no better, and this year only lays the groundwork
for the years that are to come. Listen, this is a year like no other.

This is the year the doctors struck for want of aid
and schoolchildren were sent home in the morning

and lights and gas were unreliable
and, harvesters suspect, fruit had no recourse but rot.

Many are dying for want of a cure, and the poet is patient,
and her hands cause the least of her pain.

It Is

Just before she died, she was able to ask, "What is the answer?" She got no response. Her last words were, "In that case, what is the question?"

Not who is it, are we there yet,
is anybody home. Not, how much

for the lemon? Not how much
for the ivory, the leopard,

the peach. Not, when are we leaving?
Not, how will we leave? Not, do you know

who she came with? How many clowns
will fit in the car? The head of a pin,

no one cares how many angels. No one cares
what you think of the smart bomb, corruption,

the mobs. Your opinion on deregulation:
no one's concern. The question is not

who done it. The question is not
what's for dinner, what's your beverage,

where's the beef. The question is not
who's your daddy. Is not

which way will the wind blow. Is not
where's the car. You washed

behind your ears, right? The question
is not did you turn off the oven,

did you remember to set the alarm. What's that
got to do with the price of tea in China?

Did it bite you? Did you see it? What is this?
What's got into you? No one's asking

if you know where your children are.
No one's asking if you can locate

the nearest exits. In some cases
they may be behind you. No one cares

whether or not you are being followed.
Don't ask if it makes you look fat.

The question is not
do you remember the time.

Will you, please, tell me the time?
Not, do you know the extension

of the person you are calling?
Not premium or regular.

Not, paper? Not, plastic?
Credit or debit? The question is not

what you can do for your country.
Not, now? Not, later? Not,

okay? The question is not
what your country can do for you.

The question is not who will
save us. How are you getting by?

Ease

after Carl Phillips

The difference
between To Be Comfortable
and To Be

Prosperous,
he has pulled back
the covers, called her;

he has stripped off his robe,
climbed in.

She does what she does—
presumes to be a clementine,
easy to peel, that
soon the crate,

netted, must deliver
to someone.

Is this how it will continue?
Is ease entitlement's
best reward? Is there

no withholding
what exposes itself?

At which time
she came
as if her will was his,

his will was
Spanish moss she'd pulled down
months ago and stuffed,
dry, cured,

in the summer mattress.

Rest well, she told him. Only he
wasn't tired;
he asked, *How was your day?*

A new girl
came this morning, she said,
but we won't be keeping her.

She tried her best, I imagine,

but I had to
clean up behind.

Something about Grandfathers

Fit a fastener around inside and out
twist it tight, then tighter, until intent

bulges to bursting, the way an eyeball (cartoon)
pops from the face of a strangled boy. Consider

a Christmas menagerie, complete with plastic
wise men carrying neon frankincense

and fool's gold. Gold and something
we'll call myrrh. This is how we hold on.

Because hope can satirize itself yet remain
sincere, devout. Your mother has you up before dawn

because it's Easter. Worship before eggs
and ham and all of this and that. Hold on

like this. Or some other way, say with a shoe-
box full of her father's military medals,

the slim portion of him you knew flattened in tin
and ribbon. Hold the ribbon like a subway strap

because this car *is* moves, shudders on rails
faster than a voice floating above a staircase

that belonged once to him who might call
you by that pet-name, might break you some brittle

in calloused hands were you to climb the stairs.
Hold on. Who's gone? The estimated average

is greater than one death per second. Wave
upon particulate wave, incessant. Even ritual,

which is what we have to cope with, breaks down
like candy in a fist. Faster. Soon. Even this

thought, fear not, will be gone like dust
into piles, into bins, like air from the cheeks

into a trumpet's bell, fuzzed by a mute into movement
that charges the room electric before the old man

in overalls brings out the mop. Gone like eight-tracks
wound down to a stretched out voice slowing

to crawl as a tape deck shreds tape.
After the car door closes to leave an echo

hanging in the canyon where it was shouted,
the red fields grow burred, then broken in snow.

That's a State I'll Never Go Back To

for D. A. P.

Once I got over the problem of not knowing how,
I couldn't go back to not curbing my tires, but it took awhile
to get past forgetting to register street cleaning hours,
and love, love was my handicap, though I had no permit
to hang from my rearview, so I collected seven or ten little slips
I had every intention to pay off, except I skipped town for the summer
and returned to find the guy staying in my apartment
tossed them. I'll admit I was relieved not to face these
expensive reminders of the girl I'd been, how stupid I was about life
in the city, and as I'd finished school, was moving south,
for good this time, and as I lived, then, in a state of great anticipation,
the potential of a record never crossed my mind, but now, on account
of those parking tickets, I can't go back there with a car,
though everyone who loves me knows I love that tiny window
each October in the south nub of the state you can't reach
without driving. I missed it once and waited a whole year, regretting
the lost chance to track the linden leaves' tiny migrations.
The next fall, refusing to endure that state of desolation again,
I asked everyone who loves me to please meet me, just south
of the border. We ordered green mussels. We ordered popcorn shrimp.
The shrimp beat the mussels to the table. I was the only one
who hadn't filled up on a grande egg cream—I drink for pleasure,
but since I left that state I haven't found any delicious enough to entice—
so, I ate all the mussels. Crouched, later, in that state of betrayal
that comes from learning some green things aren't good, considering
the law of averages, inertia—that any body in motion stays in motion
unless faced with an equal or opposite force—peer pressure, scatology,
the projected near-immediate devastation of world forests

46

should certain highly populated nations generally adopt

the U.S. model of toilet paper consumption, germ theory, my own role

in depressing the mean average of common human hygiene, I knew

I never wanted to be anywhere near that state again. With extradition,

with reciprocity, I was hardly away at all. When I first rolled over,

my parents were pleased and just as quickly I left the state

of never having rolled before. Ditto slumping on all fours

to crawling, and once I could walk, we all knew I was never going back.

I just pulled myself up and started moving. I grabbed at everything

I could reach. Until I learned better, I'd put my tongue on anything. Once,

I ate papaya straight from the tree and then I mourned the abject state

of the crated fruit I, living in that state, in my ignorance, thought I loved.

I denounce such love. I married a local. I taught myself how

to keep his garden. I swear: I'm staying away from that state for good.

Her mother sings warning of the new world

You will know the place
when the children run paler
                        and their mother's breasts
                                    are high
                                    with quelled milk.

                        Do not let yourself love
the man who boasts he planted each blade of the sod you admire.

                        The grass is from England, and each steer
it markets is worth more than the life of hands
whose work is to bury then raise what this Englishman takes
                        for his own.

            He will feed you well.

                        At rest in his lounge
you will taste the juice of sapodilla
            and crushed cherries.

            For this quenching,
women will forgo sleep while you dream—netted
and cool—on the white yield he allots to your body.

On the rocks

I said, the cruise line said we might see wandering albatross. I said, they said we could walk through penguin rookeries. I said, we might see at least four species of seal. What do you have against traveling where black people are? she said. That's not my idea of a nice trip, she said. My friend said, give me pink coral sand and a Mai Tai. Give me so hot men wear nothing but swim trunks, she said. Give me hot men. She said, all those days out there with nothing to do? She said, no bowling? no movies? no shops? I said, they said we would have a chance to kayak. She said I said the Drake Passage was notorious for bad conditions. I said that was true. I said, however, we'd be further south by then, in the protected bays where the Southern Ocean meets the most southerly continent. She said, oh. I said I thought if I paddled far enough from the ship I might hear icebergs melting. I said, they said we could hear gas escaping from the ice. I said, they said it would sound a bit like a soda can being slowly opened. I said I thought it would sound like what it might sound like to find myself paddling through a giant highball of vodka on the rocks, the can of tonic being opened, everything I needed right there. You wouldn't catch me out there, she said, floating with nothing but a life vest and a kayak. I said, quiet. I want to hear what quiet really sounds like.

Five for Truth

1.

Maybe you, too, have heard something but haven't seen the thing,
wondered
        longer than a moment
                at a sound that sounds like the moan of a man
losing his spleen to a gull's beak.

                It is likely only a bull seal reporting to his neighbors, but
                    you know something of seals.
        Imagine the sailor who, in 1682, saw his first seal.

                    Its bloat and bob and doggish float,
so like and unlike a water-logged man's,
   drew up a body to buoy the sound of his shipwrecked fears.

   Once,
two hours past midnight and three continents from home, I heard a wild boar rooting
just outside my camp.

                Certainly, we all have heard something we haven't seen,
        and the hearing,
        which should have been an answer,
                  has become a question
instead:

        It's wood cracking,
                under what weight?

                    It's a rock sliding,
                      where?

2.

The old man has mistaken his niece for his sister.

    And would you fault his memory its vision?
    Are you the lone one who has never confused one face with another's name?

    But it was you, remember, who mistook the other black girl for the one
your friend said you should get to know.
                    And it was you, or someone
quite like you in appearance,
              who, thinking he was somebody famous,
positioned yourself beside that no one on the train.

                    These misperceptions are nothing
          that hasn't happened before.

You've heard, perhaps, of the masseuse who gained his sight at fifty?

Everything he'd known in blindness turned into something slightly horrible
    with sight.

His cat, his dog: the animals he loved,
        the stiff or swollen limbs of clients,
            all these were varied,
                textured,
                  wonderful beneath his fingers
        but hardly differentiable,
          now,
          before his unaccustomed eyes.

3.

I have never been afraid of water, and yet I am always a little afraid
of what might be floating in it.

> Take stingrays.

> Take leeches.

> Take sharks.

Take my friend who, on the beach at age four, found a pretty thing to play with:
a Portuguese man-of-war.
> My fear is the fear of his mother seeing her son,
> his mouth almost inside the luminous jelly.

> Certain fear touches us like that,
leaving only the taste of its skin on our tongue.

Who isn't afraid of being the one disaster touches?

They say it's normal,
but the way, lately, if I pull the skin along my clavicle, it folds easily
and brings with it all that loose flesh . . .

> This is mostly all I have
to worry and be glad about:
> feeling my own body growing old.

4.

When gambling your senses, wager taste. You'd still have touch,
so you would know what textures you chewed. You'd have sight.

Like Johnny Carson, who had no taste, you'd still have your lips,
your American teeth, even, probably, your tongue.

Life is a chain of compensations.

                    My friend who drinks and smokes
and snorts the occasional powdered drug says she'll throw herself
                          from the top of a Mayan temple
when the cancer settles in.

I've seen this friend gash her forehead on the fan hung over a bar she danced on
and watched her keep dancing through the end of her tequila and two songs.

                    I wonder if my friend knows
at which stage of her ruin,
        exactly,
             she plans to let herself fly.

5.

One thing I like about the nose is how it lacks imagination.

Just last night I woke up dreaming of a body in the forest.
           No one I recognized. Maggots
busily erasing the flesh around her nostrils, her impossibly twisted arm.

Or was it alongside a road, her body?
                                        Where are we turning up
dead girls these days?

                        Fruit in her hand.

                                        Though I would not,
it was so ripe it seemed a shame to not taste it.

                                I could feel the moss she rested in
springing up after my discovering feet passed. I could imagine hearing
how she'd caterwauled in terror. In my bed, last night, I woke up, afraid
to touch her, because I knew how she would feel,
and I wanted nothing to do with that feeling.

One thing I don't like about the imagination is how it can turn against me
when I let it go.

                Let me, now please, bless my nose,
                the least creative of my organs:

Because you are, in this way, a failure,
the smell of her terror was not, this morning, in my bed.

                Bless you for not pretending to know a thing you haven't.

Bless you.

The Little Building in which I Find the Ancient Cloister
Store-room of St. Severin, which is Going to Disappear

—Eugène Atget, printing-out paper (1903)

All that will be lost has been set already into stone
from which the Madonna and her child emerged,
Mary already weeping, or perhaps not yet begun.

Centuries have torn the human features
from her face. The store-room she protects,
centuries dismantled even those good intentions.

The city turns away and concentrates
on swallows. Puddles pond the patio, reflecting
the three beams that buttress one remaining wall.

The burred trees' vernation, another unseen.
The leafing will dormant? Or finally done? The city
turns away and concentrates on mortar. In faith,

this view is but a portion of all a soul might apprehend
who wandered through the past's unkept cloister
some early hour, before the warming spring. But here,

if by here is meant now, this is all the negative, developed,
revealed. The city turns away and concentrates on all
it must desire. One gothic archway framing a window,

light crowding the left corner, overexposing the print—
gelatin silver emulsion, paper toned with broken-down gold.
Mary already weeping, or perhaps not yet begun.

before her heart, a mechanical aperture, closed

her heart, a mechanical aperture, opened;
she'd told her stomach, honey, be still;

she told her teeth and her cheeks and her tongue
all the squabbling was quail close at hand;

her heart, a perennial shrub, persisted;

she'd been waiting, she'd been waiting,
she'd looked forward to this;

she told her wrist and her waist and her ankles
all that rustling was quail in the rushes;
to the skin on her left arm, *Keep watch*,
to her lungs, *Prepare all your rooms*;

her heart, deciduous, bloomed;

she'd breakfasted on rye toast spread
with the hope sauce of bees and of thistle;

she'd been waiting, she'd been waiting;

in her rucksack she tended the first crush
of olives and, nearly transparent, delicious,
meats so rare should she share,
her heart, that tide pool, would flood;

she'd been waiting, she'd been waiting;

she told the pit of her navel and the peaks
of her nipples that cooing was quail coming near;

the call was the response she'd expected
all the days she'd looked forward to this;

though her heart, brook bed, was dammed,
she kept two small thieves, in their sockets, alert;

she commandeered all the rafts in her spine;

she'd told her heart, *Take everything*,
when he handed his hand to her hand

and the bevy, beautiful in the bushes, flew.

Post Modified Food

*

When teeth were whole and all in my possession,
I trudged across the continent to bring you back
six petals still attached the way they should be
to their stem.

*

These new seeds are non-perennial. We buy them
from the company each year.

*

Ruching in the fabric of the earth gave me pause:
Rivers. It all appeared excessive
when a simple dress would do.

*

Meals are added expenses, given the new seeds.

Fancy gowns were the first indulgence I let go.

Then I stopped buying gifts for you.

*

I doubt Lewis loved anyone.

The bitter roots between us, I had cause to reconsider.

Fair weather and, merry, I recommitted to you.

*

They said: careful, those milk teeth are coming in.

They said: stop worrying it, my dear.

They said: did you check under your pillow?

*

I ate the last orange in Nebraska.

Light like that, I got winded over the border.

*

The maize was different in every state. Harder here.
Sweeter there. Approaching blue, approaching
white, yellow, approaching green.
Still, I longed for oranges.

*

Scurvy, measles, smallpox, rickets, polio, the flu:
all the childhood and traveler's diseases. I trusted my body
to you and discovered, we ain't licked nothing yet.

*

When I found the field I wanted, I did not know
what I wanted to do.

*

We say: high fructose corn syrup, all that sugar . . .
We say: coffee, wine, tobacco stains . . .
We say: rotten. We say: dying.
We say: too hot . . . We say: too cold . . .
We say: better root it out before it's dead.

*

If they gave me my teeth back, if they cooed
and returned them with a little cash,
I would keep them in a bag—forget the meal, I'd have to
chuck the seeds, the flour, even the old-fashioned flower—
and try to bring my present back to you.

How She Keeps Faith

Dream Lake, headwaters of the Colorado

Come to the quiet time, water still in bed,
to the rock, dissimulated by the rush but still
loved.

      Stone like knees and elbows,
like fingers, the skull around eyes,

like calves, thighs, and forearms, loglong,
lying in and resting in the bed.

                  Water moving,
a body, turning as rock turns, with and against
rock.

     The meadowlong meander coming later—
the straightsurge down mountain coming soon.

    *

Here. Now. This little time
              when rock rests still in her bed.

     Before things are muddied,
               before
the turbulence recalled by walls that they have built.

Before water must confront the powerlust
of men and

        stay or be stayed

                move or be moved
by some damwill beyond her own.

                Rock
not with her anymore but always set against her.

Nowhere to run but into the field.

              Her bed
no more her bed.

    *

        Remember the first fall.

          The fall that brought her
to this quiet place,

        her body a quickcuring bruise,
first blue then green

        then clear, so flawless
veins showed through.

She is a skytear remembering.

           She is a cloudcurl
wrapped around herself.

So headheavy she falls again.

Out of the Darkness

In the beginning was the darkness.
And the darkness drew together.
And the darkness warmed the darkness.

And it was not alone.

But some of the darkness began to pull away.
The great crowd of darkness was disturbed.
This is how darkness turned against darkness.

Some of the darkness lost hair in the fight.
This hair fell to the historians, spiders. Each re-lays
the filaments just as she discovers them.

Some of the darkness lost legs in the fight.
These ran on and still dash through dreams.

Where the blood of the darkness met the sweat
of more darkness, in that place, a tree. In the tree,
some quaking possum. Below it, a hound.

Where the tears of the darkness fell, high grass grew,
through which run rivulets of an antlered herd.
Whenever darkness struck darkness, one fewer
in the herd, a new cat sprung from the grasses.

The darkness went down and the darkness rose up.
More darkness fell while some rose still.
The movement of the darkness as it fought
against darkness was like the movement of oceans.

Soon, some of the darkness was ocean.
The remaining darkness was sky.

What darkness had fallen might rise.
What darkness had risen might lose wind
and fall. This could go on forever.
The rising of darkness. Its falling.

Some of the darkness lost teeth in the fight.
These became teeth of the ancient, vigilant shark.

Some of the darkness lost nails in the fight.
These became thorns in the bramble.

Some of the darkness lost sight in the fight.
Some of the darkness lost reason.

Some of the darkness got away from the darkness.
That darkness, alone, drew a star.

My Lover Who Lives Far

My lover, who lives far away, opens the door to my room
    and offers supper in a bowl made of his breath.

The stew has boiled and I wonder at the cat born from its steam.

The cat is in the bedroom now, mewling. The cat is indecent
    and I, who am trying to be tidy, I, who am trying to do things
    the proper way, I, who am sick from the shedding, I am undone.

My lover, who lives far away, opens the door to my room
    and offers pastries in a basket spun from his vision.

It is closely woven, the kind of container some women collect.

I have seen these in many colors, but the basket he brings is simple:
    only black, only nude. The basket he brings is full of sweet scones
    and I eat even the crumbs. As if I've not dined for days.

My lover, who lives far away, opens the door to my room
    and offers tea made from the liquid he's crying.

I do not want my lover crying and I am sorry I ever asked for tea.

My lover, who lives far away, opens the door to my room pretending
    he never cried. He offers tea and cold cakes. The tea is delicious:
    spiced like the start of our courtship, honeyed and warm.

I drink every bit of the tea and put aside the rest.

My lover, who lives far away, opens the door to my room
      like a man loving his strength. The lock I replaced
      this morning will not keep him away.

My lover, who lives far away, opens the door to my room
      and brings me nothing.

Perhaps he has noticed how fat I've grown, indulged.

Perhaps he is poor and sick of emptying his store.

It is no matter to me any longer, he has filled me, already, so full.

My lover who is far away opens the door to my room
      and tells me he is tired.

I do not ask what he's tired from for my lover, far away,
      has already disappeared.

The blankets are big with his body. The cat, under the covers
      because it is cold out and she is not stupid, mews.

X

Maybe Tuesday Will Be My Good News Day

Fireflies flaring flatted fifths: I'm tuning up
on the picket fence: one moment an empty bell,
one moment a rubber mute. I've practiced
so I know what comes next. The night offers
this much and not an F more: one   then one
then two. Belfry bats could be blowing bebop
for all I care (asymmetry is obsolete . . . gone.
Gone. Gone, gone). Fire in the fire pit, the smoke
catches in his hair. The rest of the boys go on
without me, though if I wanted to chase them I could
breathe clear from the base of my belly and blow.
This isn't as complicated as it sounds, nor are those cats
in the alley scatting. I'm all tuned up and off the fence.
His solo is over and I've practiced so I know
what comes next: One/Then one/Then two.

X

Notes

"Daisy Cutter": The title refers to a controversial cluster bomb called by that name.

"On Ice": The reported last words of the English Antarctic explorer Captain Lawrence Oates, a member of Captain Robert Scott's failed polar expedition, are given in italics.

"Prayer for P——": This poem is an acrostic derived from Cavafy's poem "Prayer." I worked from a slightly altered version of the Aliki Barnstone translation found in *The Collected Poems of C. P. Cavafy: A New Translation*. The italicized line in section II is from "Chainstitching," the title poem of the unpublished manuscript by Phebus Etienne (1964–2007).

"Arthritis is one thing, the hurting another": For Adrienne Rich and 2006.

"It Is": The italicized text relays the last words spoken by Gertrude Stein.

"Ease": This poem is a response to Carl Phillips's poem "Fervor."

"Something about Grandfathers": This poem was composed in collaboration with Ravi Shankar.

"*The Little Building in which I Find the Ancient Cloister Store-room of St. Severin, which is Going to Disappear*": This title is borrowed from an image by the early-twentieth-century photographer Eugène Atget, on display at the San Francisco Museum of Modern Art.

"Post Modified Food": This poem was written for City Lights Bookstore's 2008 May Day reading, STRIKE: Igniting the Fuse of Possibility, for which some thirty poets were asked, "What serves as meaningful resistance in an age of disaster capitalism?"

"My Lover Who Lives Far": With thanks to Mahmoud Darwish.

"Maybe Tuesday Will Be My Good News Day": The title is derived from the lyrics of "The Man I Love."

Other Books in the Crab Orchard Series in Poetry